News of the World and Other Places

Poems by Jim McGarrah

ISBN: 978-81-19654-30-7

First Edition: 2024
Rs. 200/-

Rochak Publishing
HIG 45 Kaushambi Kunj, Kalindipuram
Allahabad - 211011 (U.P.) India
http://www.rochakpublishing.com
Tel: +(91) 9415091004
E-mail: info@rochakpublishing.com

Printed in India at REPRO.

This book is dedicated

To whoever reads it

Acknowledgements

Author's note: This collection of poems contains new work and a few revised poems from a much older book that is currently out of print. I am very fond of these old poems and did not want them lost. I want to say thank you to the magazines that published many of the poems in this collection for their support and confidence in my writing—26&Market, The American Poetry Journal, The Bitter Southerner, Cincinnati Review, December Magazine, Hartskill Review, Jeffereson Review, Lamar University Press, Main Street Rag, Nassau Review, North American Review, Restless (Wild Ages Press), and Vietnam War Story

Contents

Prologue: Kinship

Someone paid fifteen dollars for a book of poems
from poets around the world, and then added a crème soda

to the purchase at a place called Follet's Bookstore
in the town of Layfette, Iowa. I have never been

there, even for a crème soda. Imagine,
the body and the mind recharged with a sweet desire

to go on for less than twenty dollars.
I don't know if the first buyer was male or female,

but it makes no difference anyway.
It was enough to feel the warmth of another person.

It was enough to share their essence when I bought
the book used from a store three hundred miles away.

I found the receipt tucked between a poem
composed by Tu Fu and one by Ray Carver,

all of us separated by thousands of miles and years,
together in the instant it took to turn a page.

Part 1

"I laid my head on the railroad track waitin' on the Double E
But the train don't run by here no more, poor poor pitiful me."
—Warren Zevon

Oasis

The best shade for several city blocks
spreads itself in intermittent shadows
beneath the old oak tree next to Kroger's market.

A homeless man propped on one elbow
lounges beneath the tree parallel to a parking lot.

His body wrapped
in a filthy coat two or three sizes too large, he shelters
a dirty yellow dog that lies against the coat's lapels.

Its chest rises and falls in a regular cadence
like a worn out and wobbly piston as it pants in the heat.

A radio, once called a boom box by ancestors of the Internet,
nestles in a folded sleeping bag
blasting Calypso music loud enough to make
flies twitch and dance in feral circles around them both.

The man's unshaven face pleats in a constant smile.

Traffic shimmers by slowly
as if the whole world moved under water.

The man raises his hand to wave at each driver.
Sometimes one stops and shares a can or two from a bag of groceries.

Sometimes a driver pretends the man isn't there.

Negative Capability

An old friend asked me to give his eulogy
as if he knew death would find him first
even though we had played whiffle ball together
in my back yard when Eisenhower was president
when I pretended to hit like Duke Snyder
and he threw the holey plastic like Bob Gibson,
even though we played hide and seek with Laura
hoping for a peek at her budding breast—bragging
privilege for the winner, incentive for the loser.

We fought the same urges and gave in to learn.

We fought the same war and got high to forget.

I was angry he asked me first right to claim last rites
until I read Keats and how Keats knew this was okay.
Life is full even when we don't understand
that all living things reach a point where desire
and fear are impossible to separate. Consider oak leaves
turning skyward to welcome a hard rain knowing,
but not knowing why, it will rip them from a tree
and bury them in the soft earth.

Apocalypse

(for Bob)

The world begins
to end in Idaho
with a fishhook.

A silver trout breaks
water on the Big Lost River,
upper lip locked

onto the barbed metal
of a newly tied fly
as the sun detonates

a rainbow of diamonds
off the fish's wet back
tossing the colors across the sky.

The trout did not ask
not to be caught, nor expect
a god to save it when it was saved,

even as the god asks
this fish to forgive him
and returns it gently to the stream.

Insight

Two blocks from where I live
the School for the Blind teach people how to see.

Like bats their students steer through darkness
all the dangers the rest of us need light to dodge.

While I lie on my bed hypnagogic, still swollen
with dreams too dark to bear,

I hear the tapping of their red and white canes
on the sidewalk as they pace along not caring

if day is night or night is day, and I resent them
their blindness, unafraid as they are by shadows.

Sunday Morning Synchronicity

The worshippers of lenient gods guide
their boats from ramp to river's edge
till the brown Ohio becomes a palette,
a rainbow of mud and diesel fuel.
In go Liquid Asset, Miss Behavin', Bite Me,
Wet Dream, Hydro Therapy. What better way
to serve on Sunday than glide along
with Jesus in the wake of sunlight across
a foam of jet skis beneath heaven.
The current swirls in joy along the cutbank
and the holy hum of outboards harmonize
with the squeals of skis that ride the waves.
These aquatic conquistadores do not see,
or if they do, do not care to wave at,
a pickup truck along the levee road
as it separates bicycle from rider
and returns them both to earth in a knot
of steel and flesh. Even if a vague shiver
drifts like the mist from a passing barge
along their spines, this random sacrifice—
this propitiatory misery—is forgotten
with the next deep breath.

On Frankfort Avenue

We walk to nowhere special,
a mangy cur who doesn't care for people
and his dog, beyond Nancy's Bagel Shop,

The Reader's Corner, and one of three stores
that sell vinyl records with the hope
that being hip will make a profit. We skirt

the School for the Blind.
Dog barks at most dogs, but respects
with silence those that serve as eyes.

In front of Hilltop Tavern, a man sits alone
and sobs into the high sky. Is the airy blue
his panacea for the weight of grounded life?

Embarrassed by his tears, he and I both turn away
to hide from Dog and she, in awe of them, pulls me
down the street where she pauses at his side

listening, one ear cocked forward,
for the answer in his next salty drop to a pain
she feels without a need to understand.

Old Furniture

A gravel path splits an isolated forest.

A drainage ditch runs beside it.
Halfway between beginning and end
an old chair nests in there leaning skyward.
The chair was blue once but only patches
of its true color remain as wind and rain
have mottled the cloth with faded grays
and mossy greens after many empty days.
A child might believe ghosts are resting here.

Slight of Hand

1.

Hummingbirds stop flying
by flapping their wings.
If this lack of motion can fool
our eyes, imagine the things
we miss when we see.

2.

An armed soldier paces back and forth
at the entrance to a field guarding rows
of white crosses etched with these words:
Rest In Peace.

3.

You can hold a day.
Close your fist around the sun
until, white-knuckled, you
squeeze out a gibbous moon
and a few distant stars.
What you are left with is memory.

4.

All our gods
stand barefoot
in the snow, waiting
for flowers.

5.

The universe
exists perfectly
but does not
perfectly exist.

6.

On a rotted wooden beam
inside a covered bridge
outside of Wheeling, Indiana,
two people carved their initials
and the year, 1905. Around
those letters, they etched
these words in a heart,
love lasts forever.

7.

On Highway 41 a billboard reads
Infinity Razors – two for 19.95
Buy one. You will never need another.

8.

Main Street in Royston, Georgia:
John Deere tractors parked outside
a diner, trucks chug through town
panting rapid clouds of burned fuel,
Pentecostal, Lutheran, Baptist churches
and no taverns, three women smiling
at one child on a streetcorner who stares

skyward like an inbred snake charmer,
a single police car with a flat tire,
a post office, and at the edge of town,
a metal sign pimpled with bullet holes
"Thanks for visiting Paradise. Come Again."

9.

Flowers once ringed the oasis
around a barren town of dust
and sand called Cheribica.

Springs fed a pond
that cooled beneath the shade
of sixteen palm trees.

The flowers bloomed a vibrant red.
Their beauty hypnotized the people
who sniffed its poison pollen.

10.

On Highway 51
in rural Alabama
a sign is painted
with these words:
Jesus Died
So We Wouldn't

11.

"Body of Christ"
"Amen"

"Body of Christ"
"Amen"

"Hail Mary, full of Grace
 The Lord is with Thee"

12.

A compass always points
to the same spot called north
forty-seven miles south
of the North Pole.

13.

The world is sunlight.
We take our exercise
in a small park. Grounds keepers
prune the grass and move the goals
into place on soccer fields.
Dogs chase squirrels they never catch.
We are all thankful to be here.

14.

This morning at sunrise
as I walked a trail, I whistled.
It was a poor sound
sort of like stepping on a balloon
filled with air.

A bird replied—me once, the bird twice
and again, me once the bird twice—

We shared a deep,
primal truth. I felt like a part or nature,
not it's destroyer.

15.

This is the end.

Garage Sale

In my parents' attic
clutter metastasizes.
Cardboard urns
labeled "mixed shit" spin
in patterns, stack and rise,
crimp and crumble, bend
and split beyond control.
They contain the dead cells
of lives once lived—here,
a broken ashtray, there
a worn ball glove,
report cards and a shoebox
filled with faded snapshots
of a childhood Christmas
neither my sister nor I remember.
What use is this folded flag,
symbol for an armistice
no family reaches until death?
What we wish to be true rarely is.
Mothballs swaddle the scent
of my mother's sweater
in a musty shroud of newspaper.
Above the coos of doves
that nest in arches and a patter
of rats over rafter beams,
I imagine I hear the scratch
of a needle on vinyl from a box
of old 78s. Ray Charles singes
the air with dark blues,

as two silhouettes dance, dusty
in the yellow memory of dusk
that has slipped in through the sill
of a single window, never opened,
never used.

In the Gray Indiana Town at Dawn

Frenzied roosters echo in the valley
as shadows paint circles where streetlights die.

Used oil spit from split gaskets on coal trucks
splashing by raise rainbows out of puddles

to honor the storm that passed last night.
Cars hiss around the town square.

What night takes day does not return.
Locked stores sucked dry by Urban Sprawl

sell only shuttered memories of a time when life
meant more than gain—the pharmacy, a dress shop,

an Army/Navy Surplus, the pool hall where farmers bet
a few bucks on ball games and the bookie made great coffee.

A man emerges from an antique shop
and clutters the sidewalk with new old things

acquired from another business closing or family
escaping the stench of grain mills and boredom.

A born-again garbage man seeks god in the pink sky.
Above the clock tower on the courthouse roof, one cloud

stutters toward the dream of dawn like the boy who brings
a morning paper—news delivered, no hurry to get home.

Masters of War

1. North

Across the road, two horses buck and run, playing tag
and stopping to snack on the fescue that floors
the field in which they live. I call them Red and Blackie
for the benefit of Dog, who I named as well.

The dog can't see colors. She understands neither those words
nor the word respect but believes we all deserve respect
as neighbors who will only be neighbors once in this lifetime.
Are we masters of the world by virtue of the power in language?

The horses remind me of a photo I saw a black and white
Daguerreotype of General William Tecumseh Sherman astride
a muscular bay stallion, both man and beast next to a field
cannon.
The caption below the photo reads: *I am sick and tired of war.*

The words are owned by Sherman,
but the horse would speak them if it could see the gray
in colors—the sky blue and cloudless, trees in verdant green,
the field full of flowering clover covered by rich red dew.

2. South

At Oakland Park Cemetery in Atlanta
On a Sunday morning in June
Magnolias bloom a bitter white
flowered by silent sunlight.

Around their frail arrogance
purple hydrangeas bow in submission.
There is no breeze as I stand on ground
General John B. Hood held as he watched
while Sherman burned his beloved city.

The scent of lavender hovers above
rows of blanched gravestones
like the sickly sweetness of cotton candy
after the carnival has left the midway.
The stones stand at attention, an army
of cold marble behind Hood's cenotaph
that leads them in battle to meet the last enemy.
But here there is no sound of trumpets
no King and angels to conquer Death
only brittle bones and flesh gone to seed
in the red Georgia clay.

It was said the light of battle shone in Hood's eyes,
that he believed in cause, cross, and crown.
But, I choose to think the brightness more
a sign from flames reflected on his Quixote face,
a keen awakening that one day all the marrow
of his warriors would mingle with the dust
of his slaves buried in the plots next to theirs
as Hood's tall and thin shadow remains over them all.

3. Gods

In the Beginning
when the human race was a small thing,
like a rash on the wrist of earth, we built
our gods from clay, calling the first one Ishtar.

We gave her power over Love
bowing down before we grasped the power
of Love compelled her to make War as well.

The Truth About Mangoes

My mother called bell peppers
"mangoes" and would not stand for my correction.

The damn—a word she rarely used
for fear of sounding coarse—things were green.

She forgot they were red and yellow also,
and the fact that one grew in groves by the sea

while the other grew hollow with a lust for chili.
Nothing mattered except what her mind saw

when she heard the word "mangoes." To think
of her this way requires a constant longing.

She was the horizon,
a vanishing point, near but never reachable,

a shadow full of substance,
a ghost with flowing blood and warm tears

at the times she crushed an aspirin between two spoons
and fed it to my childish fever with a drop of honey,

or taught me how to foxtrot without tripping
before my high school prom. Hell, she even

fed my dad with silence, not speaking
for weeks when he spent a single night drunk.

A quiet life was what she valued and so returned
it to us with what she knew of love. For her fear

of feeling joy, her wish to neither brag nor complain
but bear life in silence as every godly wife was taught.

God killed her with Lou Gehrig's curse,
though watching baseball was her only vice.

Highway 41 North

The orphan's home has been demolished,
but the man next door got a new Ford truck.
A willow tree that wasn't there before
stands on the curve near an old farm
ringed by fields that lie fallow.
Grackles swirl above silos searching
for grain to glean and fill winter bellies.
The sky seems blue, a trick of the eye,
an illusion that comes from the heart.
An apocalyptic wind slings decades of dust
over the a flat unfurrowed earth existing
like bad poetry, with form but not substance.

Baling Hay

The Wabash shrinks and swells each spring.
Somewhere above flood stage, its peristaltic rage
scoops topsoil from low-lying farmland,

the current churning it into a black lava
of trees limbs and trash that may or may not
grow into hay when summer ends

if the flood fades below the river's banks
in time to seed the fields. Nature reminds us
we decide what we want, not what we will have.

One fall fifty years ago I baled hay on J.P.'s farm.
The rough timothy chaffed my forearms and the salt
from my sweat stung like a thousand tiny bees.

My brother stopped the tractor long enough to offer
a sip of tepid water from a bright orange jug.
He had knocked up J.P.'s daughter, and I was helping

pay off his shame. The crickets sang and ragweed
filled my lungs. From the forest beyond the field
a hint of honeysuckle rose and misted over us.

I felt like a man for that moment. The habit
of pretending to believe became believing.
I tossed bales from wagon to conveyor belt

and stacked them neatly in the loft, enough to feed
the stock all winter. While my brother parked
the tractor, I walked to the same river

that spilled over the field and made a lake
two months before. The sun poured its light
across the water and all my future ghosts emerged

as shadows near the bank like deer in the dusk.

Why Uncle Vern Quit Driving

Once a year my uncle rose at 3AM,
opened his first Stag Beer, and stuffed
a turkey for Thanksgiving dinner.
At noon my aunt drove him slowly
to our home where the family gathered.
It was a custom for Dad to state,
"the bird is baked and so is Uncle Vern."
We'd all laugh and I'd pretend time passed
more blessing than curse, pretend the fun
wouldn't fade. I held on to that trick of youth
as long as possible, even drove ten miles
across state lines to buy Stag beer until
it was laid to rest by corporate merger
just after Uncle Vern by cancer.
That's about when the taste went out
of a lot of things for me.
I'm sure it had to do with what I learned
at his wake, one of those mysteries unveiled
that destroys a perfect memory.
Some distant cousin told the story of Vern's
first wife, the one before my aunt that I knew
nothing about, how he drove drunk
into another car, killed her and his daughter,
and never drove again. I tried empathy,
even infused images of my recent time in war
—the blasts of mortars, the bursts of bodies,
the lessening of all life to primal urge—
on twisted metal and burned rubber.
But it did not work.

His reluctance to drive seemed
a frail repentance to me, a small gesture
for a heinous crime that lost him my respect.
I did not know then
it was the best he could do.
I did not know then
even a feather will bruise if dropped
from the proper height.

Thank Goodness for PSA's

Or public service announcements
for those the less fortunate among us
unable to decode acronyms.

Today I learned of serious danger
in morning showers. They remove
the acid mantle comprised of sweat

and sebum, a word close enough in sound
to semen that it causes raucous laughter
among less intelligent adolescents,

and even though said mantle's absence
inspires joy in odor conscious busybodies,
its presence protects from unsavory germs

as well as unwanted acne attacks.
The acid mantle's sweat and sebum form
a film like Vaseline without buying the jar.

If forced to shower from societal pressure,
it should be kept short and with cold water,
which will discourage masturbatory urges,

but bring us a healthy complexion,
even if not a robust appreciation from friends
forced to enjoy our odiferous company.

(a found poem from various billboards and in shop windows across Mid-western America shortly after September 11, 2001)

The Effects of a Terror Attack on the American Way of Life

God Bless America – Cheese Styx, $2.00

United We Stand – Cold Bud Light draft, $1.00

We Clean American Flags Free – All others $5.00

Pray for the Victims Families – Let Freedom Ring Oil Change, $12.95

Pledge Your Allegiance – Baldwin Heights Elementary School

Pay Back Is A Must – Willie's Pawn Shop

Support Our Troops – Ribeyes & Ribs Family Restaurant

My Country T'is of Thee – Sonshine Christian Book Store

We Will Prevail – American Spirit Cigaret 'tes, $3.05 per pkg.

Land of the Free – Casino Aztar – Home of the Brave

Together We Stand – Homemade Peach Cobbler and Apple Pies

Americans Against Terror – Williams and Williams, personal injury law

One Nation Indivisible Under God – Cheeseburgers, 2 for $2

What All Things Desire

"All things desire to endure within their being," - Spinoza.

It sounds simple enough, I guess. Stones desire
to be stones and tigers desire to be tigers.

I made love to a woman once who swore
she was a tree. Even the mushrooms
we ate did not confuse her words for metaphor.

She rose from atop my body with raised arms
outstretched as far as they would reach
and shook and screamed, "These are my leaves
in the wind. Watch me bend but never break."

The mountains remained mountains unmoved.
The sky changed from dusk to dawn and the wind
swung from east to west, but sky and wind
covered and cooled us both as they had before.
They endured no shift of basic intent

or indication of a transubstantiation
equal to her flight of imagination.
Her legs commenced a twitch, growing into roots.
Like a Joshua tree they reached
through soil and stone to search some distant
spring of life beyond my tactile senses.

She became more than what we were together.
Her limbs spread shelter over all existence
leaving me in the singular poverty of being human.
I sang through her tall and naked body
a song of desire composed by solar storms
and the earth's magnetic field. The birds who endured
being birds caroled as if they were a choir of angels.

My Favorite Animal

When I was a child
my mother took me to the zoo,
a place of wonder caged in sorrow.
This furry beast with duck-billed snout,
beaver's tail, webbed feet, and smaller
than a housecat, rested in tall grass
at the edge of a pond behind a wall of glass.
This beast was a crepuscular mammal,
and "with a kiss could inject venom
that caused exquisite pain," said our guide.
I had no idea what any of that meant
in the grand scheme of life until years later
when I met a strange beast of ugly beauty
with a venomous sting and called it love.

And Justice for All

Here I sit with other miscreants in small claims court,
a misdemeanor outlaw both chained to and pursued by
my own greed. I did nothing but live the Dream
till the hounds of Credit ran me to ground
as if I were a fox hiding in the subprime forest.
From the huge oak door "his honor" emerges,
black-robed prince of paupers bored by the same
bad debt complaints that tax his patience every day.
He's seen me here before and no doubt will again.
Garnishment brings me no remorse. As my old man
once said, "Ain't no use to whip a dead horse."
Blistered paint peels from blue walls as flags of both
state and nation, urged into motion by a ceiling fan,
clench and loosen muscular stars and stripes above
the bailiff who creaks for order and court decorum.
Standing straight at his honor's royal entrance, I wait
without probity for the first crook to be summoned.

Blurbing

A man named Gary wrote a story
about a war we both fought
in different parts of the same jungle.

Instead, it became one about how hope kills us.

Once he finished all the writing
and the book got bound,
Gary asked a famous writer to blurb the back cover.

You know, pen a slick review that pointed to the skill within.

Sadly, all Gary got was me.
I liked his story, not in a moral
or tasteful or happy-ending sense,

but rather in an obscene and honest war is fucked-up sense.

Gary thought my blurb fit sort of well,
like a cheap suit that he might wear
to a wedding or a cousin's funeral,

But he couldn't say how the blurb
made him feel because
he just hoped for it to be over.

You might think that Gary meant the story being over.

He didn't.

He was tired.
He couldn't eat.
He couldn't sleep.

Gary meant the present, not the past.
Waiting for a death that happened decades ago is exhausting.

The Mural on the Cafe Wall

portrays a desert wind in a mystical place
that's never been seen because it's never been.
Sand swirls across the golden ruins
of some Caliph's domed cenotaph.
Rainbows drip into an orange sunset
and onto jeweled stones. "It fosters mood,"
says the artist who also sells Turkish coffee
and rents hookahs in this college town.
She doesn't know my moods are triggered
more by memory than fluttered by art
—the rattle of gunfire and drum of mortars,
the stench of cordite, a taste of copper
in my own warm blood, and the sight
of napalm erasing whole forests.
I hear a dirge painted in her bright colors
and sung by dying prophets of many gods
arise against the spackled canvas. It moans,
although powerless to breathe, a mirage
of peace on this squandered effort
of a dissipated dream that life might mimic art,
that we might one day blend our colors
with the soft swirl and brush of touch, not bombs.

Eli's Elegy

I don't waltz or tango
fly the fly or jerk the jerk
shimmy
bop
twist
or cha-cha when the jukebox
flays the air with music
in some bayou dive, when
something inside
wants to dance its way out.

But, Eli danced
with a wide grin for all the years
we spent drinking gin, his gold
tooth refracting the dim bar light
hoping to catch a bar maid's eye
or perhaps the promise of a kiss
to ease the sadness of last call.

I can't cry for him
even though his memories
have killed him finally.
We all die from the guilt of living.
He made his choice
and was made by it when we
came home from 'Nam.
He shot his wife through the head
as she lay in bed with her lover.

I may cry once, though
and I will dance the next time
I hear his favorite
song *Bon Ton Roulet* in some
Cajun juke joint near the swamps
that he loved— wild fiddles
howling in the blue moon night,
zydeco's expelling a last spasm
of laughter at my twirling
drunken shadow—Yes.
I will dance, stumble, and cry
into a new dawn knowing no man
is ever the man he believed he *was*.

All those years
in prison sucked the rage
from his heart, and his parole
became a weight of shame,
impossible to carry with the truth
that the dead are never really dead
except to themselves.

II.

You can find poetry in your everyday life, your memory, in what people say on the bus, in the news, or just what's in your heart.

— Carol Ann Duffy

News of the World and Other Places

(*As we go sliding, sliding, sliding, sliding, sliding, sliding.... The Song Remains the Same* – Led Zeppelin)

Page 1. Headlines

Suspect arrested in connection with brutal murder of four students
Overlooked sci-fi movies worth checking out
Sailors stumble on ghost ship in Atlantic Ocean
Hunter Biden fathers child by stripper
Trump claims looking at his tax returns will harm many people
Dionne Warwick wants to meet Elon Musk
How to survive a collapsing sand dune
Where do Prince Harry and Megan get their money
Andrew Tate arrested thanks to pizza box
Low fat diet available for dogs
The truth about phlegm
Kevin solves the bonus round on Wheel of Fortune
We must save the Atlantic Right whale to save ourselves
Growing antisemitism in workplace growing
Russian officials throw tantrum when U.S diplomats call Putin a "small person"
Insurrection in Brazil

Page 2. News of Interest

At a rehab camp for alcoholics in the Catskill Mountains,
a man claiming to be the U.N. ambassador from Poland
speaks in unknown tongues to an apple tree as he brushes
the sleeves of his navy peacoat. His face as gray as the sky.

At precisely the same hour of day near a dense forest
in Germany a man lay dying in his truck
shot to death in an apparent hunting accident as his dog
sitting beside him kicked the shotgun by chance.
No animals were hurt in the incident.

Page 3. Religious Notes

The broken window is also an open one,
and the world appears in the same frame.

What we define as sin feels like salvation.

A cup leaves a circle of spilled coffee each time
the cup is lifted. The circle remains whole
only so long as the cup is in the air.

Be careful. The first beer can slip into the last call.

Page 4. Household Hints

Follow this step-by-step guide and clean your house efficiently and fast:

A. Clean the whole house, not one room at time (requires omnipresence).
   Pick one task and do it in every room in the house to fool people into thinking you've done it all.
B. Gather all your cleaning tools in a caddy, but not like the blonde caddy your husband is putting his tool in while pretending to play golf.
C. Clear the clutter.
   Go room to room and remove any children.

D. Dust and vacuum with your nose any cocaine left over from your last orgy.
E. Wipe mirrors and glass with one damp microfiber cloth followed by one dry cloth, preferably while naked.
F. Disinfect countertops and surface areas, particularly the ones that might deliver germs left over from rough sex with pool boy.
G Focus on tubs, sinks and toilets. Only you know why.
H. Sweep the kitchen and bathroom floors. Start mopping from the farthest corner of the room and move backwards towards the doorway to destroy evidence of spilled wine and semen.
I. Keep moving when you vacuum. Only a dumb ass would stand still.
J. Make cleaning a group activity (refer to orgy).

Page 5. Sports

World Gravy Wrestling Championship where men, women and children wrestle in meat juice
held in UK (interview with winner to follow after dogs finish licking him)

Page 6. Cartoons

Daily sessions of Congress
Drugs for Hypochondriacs
Fast food careers for PhD's
Joel Osteen loves poor people
Forrest Gump, President
The American Dream

Page 7. Editorial

The editors wish to commend scientists who have discovered
the virus that may soon end the world. The virus,
given the name "beinghumanitis" by a research group made up
from geniuses in the fields of sociology, anthropology, virology,
biology, ecology, psychology, phrenology, epistemology,
cosmology, geology, and most importantly, mixology
appears to have started in a garden and is well known
by its symptoms, sometimes benign but almost always
self-serving.

At a Small Mexican Diner

I saw a mule once in Matamoros,
a fine case of pastoral heterosis,
more strength than the donkey, more
pluck than the horse, smarter than either.
No species of its own, this offspring
of *Equus caballus* and *Equus asinus*,
though sterile, proved an upgrade of both.
But irate at its braying, his owner rose
from dinner with no interest in what caused
the mule's cries, only the nuisance,
and as the sun set, he shot the thing
through the head. I can't forget the sight
of that mule left to rot in dust and heat,
flies blanketing the black blood
in the unpaved street, nor how slight
the bother involved in killing
as the man returned to his meal
without even washing his hands.

Between Nogales and the Border

Prickly Pear cactus is born
as gunmetal blue fades to gray.
This remains of darkness—the decaying earth
shadows of tumbleweeds and in a soft breeze,
an echo of the world laughing. One coyote
stretches across the asphalt as an early morning
offering to the god of diesel. The beast was
slaughtered on a singular and suicidal
search for a need that will always remain
unknown—even to the coyote, especially to him.
A blue whale's song sounds at a thousand leagues.
A train whistle carries one hundred miles.
How far does the sound of death carry?
It's a fair question given how slowly
time passes through the mind that suffers.
When this coyote stood paralyzed by headlights,
the line on the road hypnotic in his eyes
like a yellow cobra swaying to the flute song
of metal, tires, and then despair, a misery
of which coyotes are mostly unaware arrived
as the hint of an unknown hunger: no more
sweet scent of desert rain, fire of falling stars,
joy of scratching for fleas or lazy stretches
in the morning sunlight, no more to see a feather
float upward or hear leaves rattle over dry sand.
The glitter, like broken glass, gone from his eyes
at the last glimpse of all he loved.

May Fourth, 1970, and 100 miles from Kent State

We are naked
the two of us and sitting
cross-legged on the mattress.

My eyes
into your eyes are blinded
by the emptiest light

I have ever seen. I don't remember
your name, only that here
the warm breath of lavender
crowds out the hint of ammonia
and cordite on the spring breeze.

The song of your breasts on my lips
begins to scream in my mind
that the moon reeks like gunpowder.

In the midst of death we make love,
an act of survival meaningless

to the ghosts passing over us.

That Time When Camus Almost Made My Head Explode

On a warm spring morning
above me a large bird wheeled
around with motionless wings,
rising and falling through air,
a wave of dark elegance
in a light blue sky and with grace
only a god or a surfer shows.
Landing atop worm-ridden
roadkill it became what it was,
a vulture, a waste removal machine
that lives because other things die.

South of Atlanta on I-75, I find America

Those rotting pear-shaped people
with their sunken chests and flesh flowing

like a feral river over the shores of wide belts,
each one with so many chins the weight of them

drags the thin-lipped mouth open in perpetuity,
I see them everywhere today, at roadside rest areas

as they walk tiny poodles with spiked collars
and in flea markets full of Civil War-flagged peanut brittle.

They offer me no apology for their misshapen shirts
and I offer none for my unkind and unfair thoughts

or the foul mood their appearance puts me in
now that I've stopped at an all-you-can-eat buffet.

It isn't that I have no pity for the gluttony I see
as the crowd of two-footed cattle rustle around

a mountain of fried chicken and a sea of gravy,
or fear, as I instinctively pat my own sagging belly.

This tragedy of corpulence isn't personal. Well,
maybe a little personal since we all appear related.

Mostly, it's metaphorical and that's where my anger
ruminates, at the point where something is

what it is not and something is not what it is. This
crowd of fat cousins has become my country, a swarm

of pasty people blanched even more by the prospect
of losing their place at the dining trough. Pushed aside

by the largest and their horrible hunger, those left behind
scratch to keep crumbs away from bus boys.

A Stroke of Luck

Mike had a stroke at the age of twenty-four.

No one—parents, friends, doctors, kin—knew
why he failed so spectacularly.

Unable to walk without aid or speak more
than simple words for the next thirty years,
Mikey labored to the grocery store, the barber,
the pharmacy, the church, and back to his home
as we all watched and clucked support.

Each step overwhelmed us with sorrow
at his bad luck. We admired his courage as he
fought his private war while secretly. We felt
lucky and continued with our own lives, staring
at office walls, standing on assembly lines,
and punching timeclocks, thankful to be whole.
We waited to end all our days with a fear
that they would never come soon enough.

The Road To

My first "real" girlfriend,
the one I thought I'd marry, the one
who wore my high school class ring
and allowed me to get to second base,
gave me a chrome exhaust extension
for my '57 Chevy on my seventeenth
birthday. Being naïve, I loved
her kind gift and did not grasp
it as a replacement for her soon-to-be
absent love. She was wiser for our age,
and knew that her offering would appease
my privileged ego. It worked, while the car
ran well and my country fought no wars.
I admit I was a shallow boy, sheltered
from memory by the safety of my dreams.

Tet Holiday in Hue, 1968

1.

Flesh floating in the fog
Blood rising in the mist
Bones waiting to be blanched
Their peace was more unfair
and yet far less cruel
than my memory

2.

Daybreak

A man sits in the door
of a Huey helicopter
that brushes
a lowland rain forest
of northern Quang Tri
—fig trees, banyans,
bamboo, and douc langur
resting on their limbs.
Beneath the broad shade
coffee farms, spiders & snails,
a white tiger with her cubs
all nest in silence
and the calm fragrance
of woodsmoke rises
from a pho fire.
Children eat breakfast.

The copter blades whir
in sync with my racing
heartbeat, rapid metallic
thumps.

The sky fills with the song
of toucans and a cry
from a harpy eagle
as fish splash in a river
running through the meadow.
Orchids bow to the wind,
as the man and twelve others
clears the copter blades
wading into what
they have flown above.
Nothing changes in the scene
as everything in the day does.

Guard Duty

1.

On those thick, hot nights
staring for empty hours
into emptiness, you always made
at least one cup of instant coffee
by boiling canteen water over
the blue flame of canned Sterno.
The brown crystals muddied
the clear liquid in the cup
as the vanishing point beyond
a boundary of barbed wire
vanished with the darkness.

2.

Time slinks through shadows,
disappears among wendigos, demons,
and wraiths that hide in mist and wait.
An unhinged hopscotch of fading light
orchestrates a symphony of sounds
until, surrounded by dark splendor
full of sightless substance, you live
like the orchids you can't see,
but you know are there. The fragile pedal
of every breath made more lovely
by resting on a calyx of fear.

Translation

He's fourteen years old and already dead,
splayed on barb wire like a squirrel on a spit.
His mother leaves the burning joss stick inside
a roadside altar close by as she carries a basket
full of balut—those fermented duck eggs
women eat in the shell that strengthen a fetus—
to sell in the marketplace.

Time is too short for incidental grief in war.
You are young compared to her, but old to death.
The smell of rotted flesh and moldy earth
no longer make you cringe as you rise
from the bunker, piss in a trough,
brush your teeth with brackish water, and listen
to her screams as if she were a peacock mating.

You load your rifle as the salmon-colored sun melts
across banyan trees, as ghosts shimmer from the hot mist
that floats above the rice paddies, as all thought dissolves
into the primal ooze of your survival. The woman wails
in a language you don't understand or care to learn.
What you came to say has been spoken and what
she answers will take you years of pain to translate.

Mechanics

The ghost of old Joe floated through
my dreams last night. He rolled a smoke
filled with Velvet tobacco and struck
a wooden match on the concrete floor.
There he kneeled in a mechanic's bay
in the back of my father's auto business
to contemplate the most efficient way
of changing a worn and wobbly U-joint
in a Dodge sedan. It was 1958
when mechanics were gods for all boys
who spent their summers loafing
in service stations or in backyards under
the shade of an oak tree in a sea of bolts,
nuts, pistons, and sparkplugs
with a fantasy of stripping an engine
and then retuning that big V-8
to a purring well-fed tom cat.
Joe proved his genius more than once
by calling for the right socket wrench
before he even knew the torque required
to tighten a loose bolt or the twist that would
smooth the pinging clack of a mistimed valve.
The example of his light touch saved me
more than once years later as I prowled
backroad bars and bedrooms indiscriminately.
Oh, I know this may seem an ambiguous
analogy or even stranger metaphor
to people unfamiliar with how the reckless

deeds of a ruined romantic might compare
to the stench of gasoline and the blue exhaust
from a burned-out engine gasket. But it does.
And here I am again. This time, I wish Joe
was around to teach me how to fine-tune
old age, how to apply just enough torque
to a rusted old bolt and not twist the head off.

Life in a Snapshot

I began to begin

I begin to have begun

I have begun to end

At the Lake

Mrs. Kaczmarek calls from her back porch
for a dog that is coupled in orgiastic delight
with Mr. Roberts' poodle near the shore.

The dog ignores her and never falters in focus.

My dad stands on the bank near a boat dock
and casts a minnow into the muddy deep.
The line arcs and the lead weight takes the bait
down where it is swallowed almost at once.

His rod bending, Dad cranks the reel, and laughs

a huge bass breaks the surface, contorting
in the air and thuds full length back into the lake.
Spray hisses and water scatters as line reels.

The sun warms his proud bearded face.

"A well-fed fish will eat a smaller one
just because it can," says dad and pats my head.
I never asked him if hunger doesn't worry
the well-fed, why the desire for more does.

Landscape Hanging on the Hospice Wall

In this painting a child squats duck-like
on a faded brick path to sniff flower petals
clustered around a magnolia bush.

I notice what my brother lying here
would call irony—a scene affirming
life hung in a place confirming death.

Our childhood was a soft cliche for us.
Holloway suckers meant to last all day,
and pitchers of lemonade under willow trees.

Our home was a place where locks
lay unused and where sharp words were
rarely needed as long as the wooden spoon

my mother used to rap knuckles remained
in view atop the kitchen counter.
The hint of dad's cigar mixed with the scent

of mom's cooking carried a sense of calm,
and fears of time passing was an illusion
and not the rhythm of regret that measures it now.

Shards of Glass

1.

In the Beginning

when the human race was a small thing,
like a rash on the wrist of earth, we built
our gods from clay, calling the first Ishtar.

We gave her power over Love
bowing down before we realized the force
of Love compelled her to make War as well.

2.

Driving by a Construction Site
where once a forest stood
I thought

What a waste
to spend our lives
always wanting something

more, the past razed
by monstrous memory,
bulldozed into a heap

of pleasant hopes
atop the future
as the present passes by without notice.

Fingers of Gods

A cyclone tore down my hometown in 1925.
The psychotic force from a heavenly source,
unlike any ever felt before, sent pigs
and cows flying. Oak trees that lined
city streets were left upturned, their roots,
raised up, naked, and garish, begging the sky
for mercy that never came.

A vortex pounded stalks of straw
into cars and trucks like ten-penny nails.
Capsized stoves in kitchens burned
homes as if they were candle wicks,
flames licking skyward as black smoke
roiled the green clouds in voracious waves.

Airborne train cars circled the rail yards,
tossed like toys over the depot as they
waited for departure. Death rode the wind
and carried the memories of forty-five people,
my aunt—sixteen-years-old— among them,
buried beneath wooden beams.

The profoundness of her loss escaped me
being years before my birth until my father
shared the story one drunken Sunday night,
and I realized the unfair and unforgiving truth.
All of us, no matter when we die, are nothing
much longer than we have been something.

Cognitive and Affective Taxonomy

A.
I never met Tim Hintz
but here's why I'd like to:
He worked the Gulf Coast waters
as a deep-sea diver, a world full
of rainbow-colored fish
and sunken Spanish treasure ships,
the place where a slight mistake
could end his life. That rush of risk
from blood to brain made every dive
a rebirth, a joy lost for me
as I sit at a desk from morning till night.

One day Tim packed away mask, flippers,
and the search for riches and moved
to Tennessee. Now, he builds
chairs from wood in the forest
near his new home, weaving
hickory bark gathered each spring
into seats that stretch across the red oak
frames and blue painted slots
he has cut and formed and hammered.
From the salt sea to a sea of trees,
he pursues the dance with each new step.
I'd like to ask him what I've missed
by thinking live meant the same as exist.

B.
I felt proud of my genius,
Lovers of my words bought me
drinks in gratitude as I regaled
crowded bars bookstores with words
that shook the walls in brilliance.
I believed my soul to be immortal
because my poems were inspired.
Then, I cupped rain in my hands
during a summer shower and watched
as it leaked between my fingers,
swallowed by the unquenchable
thirst of the dry and unyielding earth.

C.
To Do:
Order cheap cigars
Feel guilty about ordering cheap cigars
Take dog to park
Read a Borges poem
Become an eternity within myself
Wash the car
Realize I was made of stardust
Wonder where stars come from
Take out the trash before my wife notices I haven't
Reheat leftover pizza for lunch
Worry how much more my arteries clogged after lunch
Nap just long enough not to dream
Exercise to extend lifespan lost by eating pizza
Revise mediocre novel
Increase its mediocrity
Make and drink one martini
Wish I drank more

Walk past a mirror and watch my smile mock me
Read someone else's famous mediocre novel
Remember to think of what is, not what if
Be jealous that an orchid wants only to be an orchid
Be thankful for darkness
Sleep

D.
My neighbor's porch leaned inward.
After his wife died,
rails
                                        collapsed,
The floor   stripped by termites,
steps
        rotted
                        in the wet spring.
                                                        Still,
the damn thing won't fall down,
and it's fixable, like a flat tire,
a shattered window, or a bad haircut.
It takes time.
But, he never starts the work,
as if the effort's meaningless, as if
he knows that altering the present
will not correct the past, no matter
how much he wants to make it so.

E.
Today, my ex-wife bought
a pack of gum at the store
where I stopped for coffee.
Hiding behind the corn chips
and cupcakes like a shy teen

while the cashier rang her sale,
I felt embarrassed in the presence
of someone I had thought I loved.
Worn down by living, we never
sought to hurt each other. We
grew tired and then, apart.
She slipped from my grasp
as the rose petal does its calyx
when gravity is too much to bear.

F.
Twelve thousand feet:
the earth is veiled below
a translucent gauze
of smog and clouds.
Homes, like parade confetti,
line the curbed, browned
wheat fields.
The Wabash River
scrawls in looping letters
westward where it fuses
with a larger current
flowing south swallowed
by an ancient salt sea.
This is the secret beyond death,
to become fullness
in emptiness,
to mourn
the loss of shadows
when the light goes out.

The Free Will of Trees

Now, a breeze picks up
in the east and sweeps the dawn
west and with it. The flotsam
of a city night—gum wrappers,
tobacco ash, a used condom,
an empty bag, a bent beer can
with a disjointed tinkle—
follows along the asphalt curb.

As refuse of human disregard
funnels down the street,
the wind slips between
a stand of oak trees that line it.
High branches do not bow
in submission. No, they dance,
shimmy, jiggle, strut, hop

each in their own direction
with a flurry of verdant leaves.
This does not mean
the trees shiver by choice,
unless it does and joy
requires no need for meaning
in a world unencumbered
with the chains of language.

A Love Supreme

(in memory of John Coltrane)

The stench of sweat and the hint of blood
The bitter lash of a leather whip and the clatter
of chains in the dark hold of a drowning ship
The death rattle of bumble bees

—COUNTERPOINT—

The melody of nightingales

A locomotive and the hiss of steam

—INTERMEZZO—

a river spills over the blistered land
a silk scarf flutters from a barren tree branch
marbles rattle over a tin roof
nightshade flowers an intoxicating death
a crippled Trane walks around a lake six times
finally dips his toe in
polyphonic flocks of grackles score the wind
while flowers wheeze below them in the
night
and
sweet
fire
ashes of stars

insane bumper cars at an empty carnival.
Rubber trees moan in the monsoon wind
wet leaves whisper along its limbs
like a lover's fingernails in the soft coming
of spring and then, charred air.

How I Left King Arthur in Vietnam

I buried him with his magic sword
in a twisted maze of bamboo and banyan trees
pardoned from the sin of myth. This madness
of imagination died cleansed by fire and blood.

Once our battlefield was a playground
nourished by bugs and broken bottles.
With my lance, forged from a hickory stick
and sharp only in my dreams, he and I
bravely withstood the perils of attacking squirrels,
butterflies, the neighbor's feral cat
and one angry blue jay.

I held his funeral service in a place
called Quang Tri, the scent of napalm
filled the air, and the burning cloud formed
a tribute before the heavy rainstorm.

Apostasy

Someone gifted my dying mother
a set of hands carved from soapstone
and raised in prayer on a soapstone base.

A slight flick of the switch in the base
flooded the hands with jaundiced light
all the way up to the tips of their fingers.

For weeks, I sat at her bedside turning
that bulb off and on. Each time, the hands
reached upward for what wasn't there.

Extinction

The last DoDo bird died
In the year 1692.
We have only a portrait
to approximate its appearance.
The poor things began
their demise when their young
got fat and happy.
Then, they forgot how to fly.
The last of this species, named
the White DoDo, expired
because of what avian experts
call human involvement.

Ballet

The Dying Swan is a movement most favored
by the dead, plies, jetes, and pirouettes performed
with an insane amount of balance and technique
that hides the fear and pain in finally getting there.

You spin on one leg, like a twirling top,
as you leave the audience in their tears,
as your body bends and twists, swirling on the tips
of five unsubstantial toes in a motion

controlled by the dignified stiffness of acceptance.
There is no grand pas de deux except the one shared
by those who watch this, the finale—buoyant and fluid—
soon to be shared with them all.

Caged

(an homage to Rilke's poem, "The Panther")

Maybe we got things wrong.
What if the panther climbed
into its cage on purpose, not
as an object to amuse children
with a display of primal rage
but to temper its own disgust?

Maybe the panther did not want
to escape and its steely-eyed stare
Rilke described with painful detail
was not caused by the misery
of captivity, but a gaze of regret
for the sad beasts that milled around it.

Epilogue:

Coming Home

Early Days

He knew that he needed to be held. Part of his mind ordered him to bring someone close, stroke her hair, feel her heart and his beat together. Part of his mind recoiled with the fear of being touched, and this was the strongest, loudest, angriest, most hopeless part. The closer you bring someone to you, the farther you push them away. He had nothing to say. The physical power of words had been lost. Larger voices called, the hum of the fan in their bedroom, starlings whistling outside the window, a hungry cat squalling from the alley, the dead lying in dark back rooms and streets wiped clean of carnal attachments. Reality was only a lace curtain seen through when you weren't even looking, easily ripped apart and separated by time and space, connected by the thinnest of threads, but mostly a veil. He knew words existed, but his language was now different from the rest of the world. It rained before dawn and he tried to count the drops as they—one two three—as they exploded against the windowpane into infinity. He had accepted death to survive.

He was no stranger to irony—the hospital built next to a ski lodge, the biggest bass he ever saw broke water and snapped his line, his ex-wife married their divorce lawyer, his best friend's only sins were venial and the man confessed once a week, prayed constantly and killed no one even while at war.

He did not believe in any god himself, until that day when his squad gathered at the edge of the dense and dark jungle where the rice paddies ended. The mortar shell fell through the gloaming and after it fell, left only the silence of his friend in the stench of jasmine, cordite, and blood. Then he knew that God was the Terror of living.

Therapy

Framed by degrees books computers and a broken clock his doctor sits amid this refuse of her clinical kingdom explaining the bond between the squeeze of a trigger and the rush of blood through the brain, the pain with joy as if you swallowed a whole bowl of ice cream all at once. "That is one inconsistency of war to men of good conscience." But she did not understand. No one knows, even an artist, what the primal mind chooses for its art—foreground, background, contrast, form, and substance—There is no search for sense in his thought anymore. Memories that bleed the brightest colors seek him out.

Blending In

In his favorite diner in his hometown in the early morning after coming home, he drinks his bitter coffee. The man at the counter on his right reads the news with feigned interest as if the print might be a bite of unbuttered toast. An old couple chew their scrambled eggs slowly like cows waiting for a truck to the abattoir. A young man in a white tee-shirt speaks with animated gestures to a forlorn waitress. Three grandmothers stuff their grandkids with pancakes and syrup. Outside the large window the sky folds over the highway as traffic comes and goes. The ebb and flow of ordinary life goes on while somewhere in his mind a bullet rips into flesh, a child lays across the unmoving corpse of his mother, jets whine low in the sunrise and the jungle explodes in fire. The scent of bacon and the clank of spoons against ceramic cups surrounds the room with a routine of life that has no knowledge of random death. Montaigne discovered four hundred years ago that nothing makes us remember it so well as the desire to forget it.

Re-Education

begins by counting ceiling tiles during a lecture on fossils. Semoria is a reptilomorph named for a town in Texas. Winged lizards nested on the ground, unlike bats. Straight-ankle thedodants evolved into crocodiles and then, humans. He is learning these facts because his therapist told him education is the key to becoming a civilized human. In fact, he had known a thecodant in DaNang with perfect ankles. Her neck smelled like jasmine and vanilla and sweat. He paid her a dollar extra so she would whisper the name of his high school sweetheart as he came. He chose "Karen."

"Anapsids, synapsis, diapsids all may have been warm-blooded," the professor's voice echoes along the classroom walls and his disconnected shadow flutters along with it under the blanched flicker of the overhead lights.

The young woman in the seat next to him is warm blooded, and she is no fossil. She smells like honeysuckle, her hair is a blonde curtain that must be gently parted with his fingers to reach her thoughts. Her sighs of boredom distract him. They sound like spring rain kissing a small lake.

"Vocalization among dinosaurs would strongly suggest social interaction," The professor chants his monotone mantra beside the blackboard. 'Some cataclysmic event ended their reign over the earth. All that we have left are fragments of their bones."

What if dinosaurs died during TET in 1968, littering the city of Hue with their bones as the streets filled with smoke and the stench of cordite burned his nose. He sits quiet among other students, learning that some knowledge is best kept to himself and so, pretends to be an actor in a great play who has been inspired not as much by character or plot, as the numb vacancy in his mind and a talent for being what he is not.

Redemption

Dawn began to sneak through the breezy cracks in the old farmhouse as the amphetamines wore through his brain. Sunlight and shadows hopscotched across the furniture and floor. Hours must have passed in the cloud of smoke from burning cigarettes. His voice sounded like wet sandpaper on metal. No one had moved away from the group gathered for his confession. A woman held him and the rest of his friends sat at his feet. He began to feel empty. The oil of his being poured out on the heads of disciples, anointing them with his infinite knowledge of philosophical treatises, theological mythology, sociological ramifications, and feral theories on the fall of man in war. He stood and took the woman by the hand and spoke no more. They climbed the stairs in the old farmhouse. They made love and slept. When he woke, it was twilight of the same day. Cold and alone, even with a warm body beside him, the idea that he might be dying crowded into his thoughts. Opening the only window in the room, he crawled out on the roof as the sun folded itself into the earth. Blackness began to creep forward from the horizon, covering the gray so slowly he could feel the planet rotating on its axis. The spring warmth came apart like wet newspaper and the air chilled. The smell of dead flowers overwhelmed him, and he didn't know where it came from. The lilacs and tulips had yet to even bloom. He sat wondering if they ever would.

www.ingramcontent.com/pod-product-compliance
Lightning Source LLC
Chambersburg PA
CBHW022201160726
48282CB00024B/277
* 9 7 8 8 1 1 9 6 5 4 3 0 7 *